SUCCESSFUL
SPORT MANAGEMENT

Edited By
GUY LEWIS
HERB APPENZELLER

THE MI
La
CHARLO

INTRODUCTION

By

Guy Lewis

Sport management has existed as an activity from at least the time of the ancient Greeks, reflecting the importance of sport in the lives of men. Sport management in modern times, however, has not developed professionally as rapidly as management in other industries, perhaps reflecting a continuing association in the public mind of sport with play and management with work. Effective operation of sport-related activities is, nevertheless, essential for the pleasure of players and spectators alike and for maintaining the cash flow that makes this pleasure possible. *Successful Sport Management* draws on the experience of more than twenty professionals to provide, in a single volume, a reference manual for all those whose responsibilities include management of sport and associated business. The key element in the development of a professional field is a body of knowledge, a literature rich both in volume and substance. While this volume is not a work in which the subject matters that make up the field of sport management are exhaustively described or perfectly integrated, it does highlight the substance of an increasingly important literature and hopefully, by so doing, contributes to the definition of the discipline of sport management.

Successful management is essential to all segments of the sport industry, professional or amateur, school or club, private or government at any level, community or individual. Whatever the location of the management function, the same basic requirements are present: namely, effective and efficient management of personnel, program, marketing, information, facilities and legal responsibilities. The six parts of this work are devoted to these topics. Selected general documents are included in the individual chapters to enable a manager to draw new elements from his or her operating philosophy.

Within each part the chapters follow a logical order dictated by the management function. Part 1, *Personnel Management,* begins with a consideration of the contribution of recruitment and training to the development of an effective staff, continues with a discussion of time management, and concludes with techniques for dealing with stressful situations. Part 2, *Program Management,* covers development of program philosophy and objectives, the mechanics of scheduling, budgeting and financial management, equipment control and provision of medical services for teams and/or spectators. Part 3, *Marketing Management,* begins with a description of the characteristics of sport marketing and then suggests ways of marketing events, marketing services, raising funds, and increasing ticket sales through promotions, and focuses attention on internal marketing. In Part 4, *Media and Information Management,* the discussion of public relations is extended, the benefits of computer applications to sport management tasks are assessed and the impact of options in the use of television is measured. Running throughout this section is attention to the question of media relations.

Part 5. *Facility Management,* poses and answers questions concerning contractual arrangements among sponsoring agencies and host facilities, the philosophy of operating a public access facility, the management of individual events, and the internal ongoing management of activity centers. Part 6, *Legal Management,* provides an introduction to risk assessment and reduction, specific terms of contracting with participants, suppliers and staff, an individual chapter on team sport contracts and an overview of the law pertaining to public assembly facilities.

Those who choose to read *Successful Sport Management* as a single work rather than as a series of topical chapters will find that there is some material common to several of the chapters. This is inevitable, both because the chapters are intended as stand-alone units and because some principles of management are constant from setting to setting. This measure of overlap also suggests, however, that professionals independent of each other in their day-to-day operations increasingly find common ground in defining the essential problems and strategies of sport management. The editors and authors hope that, as the body of information on sport management increases, the arrangement of that information can become increasingly precise through conferences and additional publications. When this happens, sport management will take its place as an appropriately recognized branch of the management field.

ACKNOWLEDGMENTS

The editors wish to express their gratitude to all who contributed to making *Successful Sport Management* available to the many professionals who work in the field. The authors not only accepted and met deadlines but reordered personal schedules to give each chapter continuing attention as it was prepared for publication. Deborah Parda and her staff, Eileen Farr, Ann Flanagan, Dana Giampa, Kevin Heman, Tracy Lane, Marlene Makie and Satoko Motouji, provided the effort behind the scenes without which no editor succeeds. Caroline Gouin was tireless in proofreading revisions and Millie Dunkel typed and retyped numerous materials. Finally, particular thanks goes to Professor James F. Gifford, Jr. of the Duke University School of Medicine for suggesting numerous ways to improve the agreement of structure within and between chapters and to enhance the quality of individual chapters. Without his assistance the volume would have been less readable and less useful as a reference tool.

Guy Lewis
Herb Appenzeller

TABLE OF CONTENTS

PART 2

PROGRAM MANAGEMENT

PART 3

MARKETING MANAGEMENT

PART 4

MEDIA AND INFORMATION MANAGEMENT

PART 5

FACILITY MANAGEMENT

PART 6

LEGAL MANAGEMENT

ABOUT THE AUTHORS

HERBERT APPENZELLER
Director of Athletics and Professor of Sport Management
Guilford College

Herb Appenzeller is Professor of Sport Studies and Athletic Director at Guilford College. He is the author of six books in the area of law and sport and co-author of *Sports and the Courts Quarterly*. He is the Executive Director of the Sports Studies Foundation.

JOHN BILLING
Chairman, Department of Physical Education
University of North Carolina/Chapel Hill

Prior to his tenure at The University of North Carolina, John Billing held similar administrative positions at The University of Connecticut and The College of Santa Fe. Responsibilities at these institutions have included personnel development, curricular revision, budget management and facility supervision. He has taught courses in Administrative Designs for Sport and Physical Education and a Seminar in Sport Administration. In addition, he has designed, administered and consulted on special projects with groups as diverse as the Connecticut Commission on Fire Prevention, Xerox Corporation and Nuclear Security Forces.

WILLIAM T. BROOKS
William T. Brooks & Associates

William Brooks is one of the nation's most highly sought after speakers, trainers, and writers in the areas of time management and personal productivity. He annually conducts in excess of 150 seminars from coast to coast. An honors graduate of Gettysburg College, where he was an All-East football player, he also holds a masters degree from Syracuse University. A former college football coach, university dean and instructor, he now heads his own firm specializing in seminars, workshops, consulting, and professional speaking. William Brooks' clients range from Fortune 500 firms to professional athletic teams, educational institutions, and every imaginable organization that is seeking to improve the performance of its most valuable asset — people.

DON CANHAM
Director of Athletics
University of Michigan

Don Canham has been Michigan's Athletic Director for the past 16 years. He has served on a multitude of Big Ten Conference and NCAA committees, including the all important NCAA Television Committee. He has also been called as a consultant and advisor to 11 major institutions in the last 10 years. A coach for 15 years and a business major, Canham has the ideal background for an athletic administrator. Canham has spoken throughout the country to countless business groups and associations on marketing, promotion and business practices. Recently, he has become highly involved in pay and cable television and has served as a panelist at major marketing seminars.

During the last 16 years Canham has earmarked more than $10 million from athletic receipts for plan expansion and improvements. Additionally, he was a key mover in the $7.2 million construction of new recreational sport facilities that gave Michigan one of the largest indoor complexes in the nation (333,000 square feet).

Michigan's intercollegiate program includes 21 varsity sports for men and women with an annual budget of $14 million. The department, as stated, is self-sufficient and has never used state, federal or University funds for building or operations.

GEORGE DANZIGER
Department of Sport Studies
University of Massachusetts/Amherst

George Danziger's first exposure to computers was during summer employment while a college student in 1964. As a statistical clerk, he assisted in the administration of large scale (3000 cases), long-term (10 years) longitudinal study using punched cards, card-tabulating equipment, and, what were then, very advanced desk-size, programmable calculators. In the course of undergraduate and graduate studies in anthropology, Mr. Danziger broadened his statistical analysis, and Fortran programming of large-scale mainframe computers.

After leaving Columbia University in 1970, Mr. Danziger worked as a consultant to numerous small (under 100 million annual sales) manufacturing firms. His primary focus was identifying areas for computer applications, and training of personnel to implement and operate computer systems. He also wrote custom software for inventory and production control on mainframe computers. He has also started and continues to manage his own manufacturing firm which produces precision electro-mechanical clutch and brake units for use in copying machines, bank vaults, and robotics. He has also published software for the home computer market.

Since joining the faculty of the Sport Management program at The University of Massachusetts in 1983, George Danziger has devoted his attention to teaching courses on the effective use of microcomputers in Sport Management. His own continuing research in the area is aimed at developing simplified methods for using "off-the-shelf" software to tackle common sport facility management problems such as workforce scheduling.

LYNNE GASKIN
Professor of Physical Education
University of North Carolina, Greensboro

Lynne Gaskin received her B.S. degree from Wesleyan College in Macon, Georgia, and her M.S. from The University of North Carolina at Greensboro where she currently is completing the requirements for the Ed.D. Miss Gaskin has taught in the Department of Physical Education at The University of North Carolina at Greensboro since 1966, and her work has been focused primarily in the areas of teacher certification, coaching preparation, and the legal aspects of sport and physical education. She has been actively involved in a variety of professional associations at the state, regional, and national levels. Publications and program presentations have been centered on professional preparation of coaches, alternative careers in physical education, and the implications of Title IX for coaches, teachers, and administrators.

JERALD HAWKINS
Chairman of the Department of Sport Studies
Guilford College

Sport Medicine coordinator for the athletic program at Guilford College. Jerald Hawkins is a certified athletic trainer and exercise physiologist. He is a member of the National Athletic Trainers Association and American College of Sports Medicine. He is the author of several publications on sport injury management, personal fitness and exercise physiology, including his role as editor and contributing author of *Sports Medicine: A Guide for Youth Sports.*

DAVID KLATELL
Director, School of Journalism
Boston University

David Klatell also founded and serves as Co-Director of The Institute in Broadcast Sports, a research center specializing in the business relationships of television and sport. In addition, he teaches television sport management at the University of Massachusetts. David Klatell maintains an active professional consulting practice in media services and frequently addresses convention audiences and other groups on the subject. He is the author of numerous articles, and co-author of *Television, Sports and Society,* to be published by Oxford University Press. He holds degrees from Wesleyan University and Boston University.

GUY LEWIS
Head, Department of Sport Studies
University of Massachusetts/Amherst

Guy Lewis is president of the Sport Studies Foundation. Sport Management at the University of Massachusetts has been at the forefront of developments in academic preparation for careers in sport management. Innovations include development of coursework specific to management of operations and organizations in the sport industry, a faculty possessing academic qualifications necessary to the generation of meaningful course contents in sport management, and the establishment of courses of study leading to BS, MS and PhD degrees.

CHESTER LLOYD
Consultant

Chester Lloyd is a specialist in the delivery of emergency medical care for mass gatherings and/or large facilities. For the last ten years he has been involved with the planning, training, and patient-care aspects of emergency medical services. His experience included work as a coordinator of emergency medical teams for a large-capacity stadium. Chester Lloyd completed his Master's of Science degree at the University of Illinois, Urbana-Champaign, where he researched emergency medical preparedness at mass gatherings. Currently, as an independent consultant, he provides advice on emergency medical response in entertainment and sport facilities, in corporate offices or industrial settings, and at any facility or event which attracts large crowds.

CHARLES LYNCH, JR.
Partner in the law firm of
Keziah, Gates & Samet

Charles Lynch, Jr., is a graduate of the University of North Carolina and the law schools of the University of South Carolina and New York University. The major focus of his law practice is on matters of corporate and tax law.

GEOFFREY MILLER
Director, Physical Education Center
Guilford College

The $4 million Guilford College Physical Education Center serves during a given 12-month period some 4,500 individuals. Use of the building ranges from infants learning to swim, college students and YMCA members. His undergraduate studies were completed at Amherst College, and he earned his master's degree in Sport Management at the University of Massachusetts in 1979. The current position was accepted in

1980. Additional responsibilities include head coach of lacrosse and Assistant to the Director of Athletics.

PATRICIA MILLER
Associate Director of Athletics
Harvard University

Patricia Miller is responsible for satisfying the needs of both the men's and women's programs. Her specific assignment is to serve as scheduling officer for the Department of Athletics. She is Secretary of United States Olympic Committees (U.S.O.C.) Education Counsel, and a member of U.S. Women's Olympic Rowing Committee.

JOHN MOORE
Associate Sports Information Director
Duke University

John Moore began his present appointment a few months after graduating from Guilford College. During his undergraduate days he served as Guilford's Sports Information Director for three years. His responsibilities at Duke include extensive involvement in promotion and advertising.

DAVID MORELLI
University of North Carolina/Chapel Hill

David Morelli has been an equipment manager on the high school and collegiate level for twelve years. He is presently the equipment manager for football at the University of North Carolina at Chapel Hill. He is a member of the Athletic Equipment Managers Association and the Advisory Board for the Nike Company.

BERNARD MULLIN
University of Massachusetts/Amherst

Bernard Mullin is Assistant Professor of Sport Management and Marketing, Department of Sport Studies, University of Massachusetts, Amherst and President of National Sport Management, Inc., a sport marketing and management consulting firm. Dr. Mullin has published several articles on Sport Marketing and has recently completed work on a manuscript entitled *Sport Marketing, Promotion and Public Relations,* published by Burgess Publishing Co., Minneapolis, Minnesota. The book in workbook form has been adopted by sport management programs at several colleges and universities.

Bernard Mullin is considered by many to be the foremost academician in Sport Marketing, and has been recognized for his pioneer research in the use of sport as a marketing tool for business and industry, by local and national media, such as the Washington Post and NBC on national television (NBC TV's — *First Camera* program) and even in the International Press in such diverse mediums as Rolling Stone magazine.

Bernard Mullin holds a B.A. Business Studies from Lanchester Polytechnic, Coventry England; and M.S. Marketing a Master's in Business Administration (MBA) and a Ph.D. Business Administration from the School of Business, University of Kansas.

Dr. Mullin's client list includes organizations in professional sport, intercollegiate athletics, tennis, racquetball and fitness clubs and resorts. He has been invited to present seminars in marketing and public relations at Major League Baseball's Winter Meetings, and numerous local and national conventions of sport associations such as the Intramural Association and the International Racquet Sports Association.

Prior to coming to the U.S.A., Mullin played for the Oxford City Football (soccer) Club in England, and spent several years in executive positions with the British Leyland Motor Corporation and Serck Tubes Limited.

JAMES OSHUST
Managing Director
Greensboro Coliseum Complex

James Oshust's career in facility management began with an appointment as General Manager of the Sioux Falls, South Dakota Arena and Coliseum Complex. He also served as Promotion Director, Toledo Sports Arena. Other appointments have been as General Manager of the Niagara Falls Convention Center the Mid-South Coliseum, Memphis, Tennessee. He is a graduate of Ohio State University's School of Journalism (Radio-TV News), and has served as publicity representative for Holiday On Ice Shows, Inc. He has also worked in commercial television production. At one time he held the offices of Executive Vice President and General Manager of the St. Louis Stars Professional Soccer Club, North American Soccer League. He is a member of the Board of Directors of the International Association of Auditorium Managers.

AL RUFE, JR.
Associate Athletic Director & Business Manager
University of Massachusetts/Amherst

Al Rufe served as Business Manager only from 1968-1975. A graduate of Mt. St. Mary's College in 1965, Al Rufe received a Master's Degree from Boston College in 1967 in Business Administration. While at Boston College, he served as varsity soccer coach. As an undergraduate, Rufe was a member of Mt. St. Mary's varsity soccer and track teams earning all conference and all South honors in soccer. During his tenure at the University of Massachusetts, he served as the varsity soccer coach from 1973-75. His current responsibilities include all financial aspects of the athletic/intramural department and scheduling for intercollegiate athletics and personnel management.

FRANK RUSSO
President, Monitor Productions, Inc.

Monitor Productions (a Bronson & Hutensky Company) presents sporting, entertainment, and tradeshow events. Monitor also provides consulting services to the arena/convention center industry. Frank Russo is the former Executive Director of the Hartford Civic Center (1976-1983) where, under his leadership, that facility achieved a schedule of over 600 event days per year, annual gross ticket sales in excess of $15 million and an unprecedented cash surplus of $1.2 million in the fiscal year 1981-82. Frank Russo is also a Lecturer at the University of Massachusetts, Department of Sport Studies where he teaches a course in Spectator Facility Management. He holds a B.A. from St. Michael's College and an M.A. (Public Administration) from the University of Connecticut.

JOHN SWOFFORD
Director of Athletics
University of North Carolina/Chapel Hill

John Swofford has been Director of Athletics at the University of North Carolina since May, 1980. In that position, he oversees one of the most successful and best-balanced athletic programs in America. Carolina football and basketball teams are traditionally ranked among the Top 20 in the nation and the Tar Heels also field outstanding teams in non-revenue sports. Swofford was appointed to the NCAA Football Television Committee in 1982 and served as chairman during the time the issue of football television rights was under dispute in the courts. A native of North Wilkesboro, N.C., John Swofford was a Morehead Scholar at North Carolina and a quarterback and defensive back on the football team. After graduating in 1971, he attended Ohio University where he earned a masters in athletic administration.

JEANEANE WILLIAMS
Director, Public Relations & Publications
Guilford College

Jeaneane Williams began her career with an appointment as the first female sports editor for the Altamahaw-Ossipee (North Carolina) High School newspaper. She has been an associate editor and promotion supervisor for McGraw-Hill Book Company and director of advertising and promotion for another publishing company, Garrett Press, both in New York; editorial services director for Colorado magazine in Denver; and has worked for the University of Colorado and the University of North Carolina-Chapel Hill in technical editing, writing and development. She holds a B.A. in English from the University of North Carolina-Greensboro and has done additional work in her field at the University of Colorado and at New York University.

GLENN WONG
University of Massachusetts/Amherst

Glenn M. Wong is an Assistant Professor in the Sport Management program at the University of Massachusetts/Amherst. He has written several articles in the sport law area and has co-authored a sports law book entitled *The Law and Business of Sports*. The book has been accepted for publication by Auburn House Publishers in Dover, Massachusetts and the publication date is 1985. Professor Wong teaches Sport Law, Sport Finance and Business and Sport Labor Relations at the University of Massachusetts. Attorney Wong is a member of the Massachusetts Bar and the American Bar Association's Forum Committee on Entertainment and Sports Law, for which he chairs the Subcommittee on Sports Bibliography. He also serves on the Massachusetts Governors Council on Physical Fitness and Sports. Attorney Wong received his undergraduate degree from Brandeis University in economics and earned his law degree from Boston College Law School. Other professional pursuits of Attorney Wong include the negotiation of a number of contracts for professional athletes in football, basketball, baseball and soccer.

Part 1

PERSONNEL MANAGEMENT

Chapter 1

STAFF RECRUITMENT, SELECTION AND RETENTION

By

John Billing

§ 1-1. Introduction.

Personnel constitute the primary resource of any organization. The goal of personnel management is to obtain competent employees and provide the means for them to function optimally. Sport organizations are people-oriented operations, consisting of persons as producers, as products and as consumers. This contrasts to many other businesses that deal with raw materials, automated machinery and indirect public sales. The fact that sport organizations are so people-oriented elevates personnel management to a primary function in organizational management. In addition, the human problems of management are often the most complex due to the variability of human nature and behavior. Therefore, the management of the personnel resources of any sport organization is paramount to the success of the organization.

§ 1-2. Personnel Management Defined.

Personnel management involves all the ways in which employees interact in both the formal and informal context of the organization. Typical aspects of personnel management include:

1. Obtaining competent employees;
2. Assigning them effectively;
3. Motivating them to perform optimally;
4. Stimulating their professional growth and development;
5. Evaluating and compensating them fairly; and
6. Retaining or dismissing them.

The decision to employ a person is an extremely important undertaking. Making a poor hiring selection costs the organization in many ways. Employees represent a substantial financial commitment when viewed over their entire career. The cost in time and effort to recruit and train the new employee is substantial. In addition, the unpleasant consequences of having to dismiss an employee and the resultant bad feelings and potential loss of productivity until a replacement is found are all negative results of poor employee selection.

§ 1-3. Professional and Hourly Employees Defined.

Since sport organizations are people-intensive operations, every staff selection is of primary importance. Normally, organizational personnel are classified as either professionals or hourly employees. Professional employees are those occupying higher-level positions in the organization and who do not have fixed work schedules, do not punch time clocks or have highly defined benefit packages. They are expected to perform specific duties for the organization that are not directly linked to a fixed day/hour work schedule. Hourly employees, by contrast, usually have very specific day/hour schedules, often are required to keep records of their work time, may have specified lunch and break times, receive specified vacation time and sick leave and are not expected to work "after hours" without additional compensation. In general, administrators, managers, coaches, public relation officers and similar appointees are considered professional employees. Secretaries, ticket office employees, equipment managers, janitors and security officers are considered hourly employees. The hourly employees may be considered support personnel to the professional segment of the organization.

§ 1-4. Place of the Organizational Chart in Staffing.

All staffing selections must begin with the administrative organizational chart. This chart should clearly depict the lines of authority and responsibility of the various members of the unit. The chart identifies the basic structure of the organization and where each employee fits into the scheme of operation. All employees should be familiar with this chart and understand how their positions and duties contribute to the composite structure.

§ 1-5. Job Description.

Each position within the organization should be explained in a job description which details the major responsibilities, who the individual is responsible to and who he is to supervise. The job description should be in sufficient detail to succinctly portray the essence of the duties. The composite of all the position descriptions for the organization details the total assignment of responsibilities and serves as a means of communicating the formal operation of the unit. (Example is located in Appendix 1 at the end of this chapter.)

§ 1-6. Position Announcements.

Position announcements are public advertisements of positions to be filled. They should be carefully constructed to depict the primary duties as identified in the organizational position description and should also include information on appropriate qualifications, salary, benefits, starting date and how to apply. Many organizations now require extensive advertising of openings including direct mail announcements to educational institutions and to similar organizations, newspaper advertisements, listings in appropriate placement services and at professional meetings. In many sport organizations word of mouth remains a primary mode for communicating position openings. Administrators from one sport team or athletic department ask their friends in similar organizations if they can suggest appropriate candidates. The recommendation from a highly respected colleague is often the most important credential a candidate can possess.

A reasonable time period should be provided after the opening is announced before closing the search for a professional position. This allows sufficient time for candidates to learn of the opening and submit their applications. An exception to this practice is often employed when selecting new head coaches. Many times a very short period is all that is provided and only a few pre-selected candidates are considered. This is considered necessary to prevent the disruption which would occur with a lengthy search process.

Usually a selection committee reviews applicants and selects several as the most promising candidates. These finalists are often invited for a visit which allows the candidate to see the new situation in person and for numerous interviews with officers of the organization. The qualifications of each finalist should be thoroughly checked for accuracy and their references contacted. Often the materials submitted as the position application will be vague as to the actual duties which the applicant performed. A check with former employers and references can confirm the exact nature of a candidate's former duties and how effectively the duties were performed. Many positions are formally filled with the signing of an employment contract. Others involve only a letter of appointment or a standard employment form. In all instances, some official employment document should be signed by both the employer and employee. The employee should also receive written notification of all benefits which are provided as part of the employment.

§ 1-7. Recruitment — Cautions and Strategies.

An important question to be answered when filling positions is whether it is desirable to fill the positions from within the existing staff via promotion or transfer or to seek outside applicants. It is the philosophy of many organizations always to look within to promote loyal and competent employees as a preference to bringing in new outside personnel. This practice has the advantage of building staff morale and a conscious effort by employees to achieve and thus earn their way to more desirable positions. It rewards loyalty and provides a strong base for tradition and standardization of operation. However, many outsiders may have qualifications superior to any current members of the organization. They will be more likely to provide new ideas and approaches to their assigned duties. In most instances, it is best to solicit applicants from both within and without the organization. Careful judgment will then produce the best selection from the potential candidates.

§ 1-8. Staff Training.

The training of personnel consists of the entire spectrum of job development beginning with familiarization of the new employee to the organization and his duties, specialized on-the-job training, career development and retooling. The employee should see this process as career development designed to make the employee a more effective member of the organization.

It is essential that new employees be assimilated into the organization with minimal stress to the employee and the ongoing operation. This is best accomplished by some means of formal or informal training. Specific mechanisms should be in place for introducing the new employee to the job duties and the important items of "how it's done here." Often a specific supervisor is charged with providing this introductory information. This process also happens informally with interaction among co-workers. Established employees should be encouraged to help "educate" the new employee and all other employees should be tolerant and understanding of the minor errors a new employee is likely to make. New employees should be specifically encouraged to ask questions about anything which is unclear and should also feel they have someone to turn to during this introduction period of employment.

Many positions in sport organizations require some on-the-job training to familiarize the new employee with specific equipment, machinery or facility operation. Specific plans to provide this knowledge and experience must be a part of the orientation of new employees on the staff of most support units including: janitorial, maintenance, grounds crew, lighting and media crews and security.

Career development is the long-term commitment of the organization to the improvement and advancement of its employees. Opportunities are often provided or encouraged which allow employees to upgrade their skills, increase their education and acquire new abilities which might contribute to their current job performance or qualify them for advancement. Some organizations will make these opportunities available free of charge or grant released time for career development. Others may pay a portion of the cost or merely encourage persons seeking advancement to acquire the additional skills. A current example is the need for employees at many levels to become familiar with computer capabilities. Many records are now being computerized. Ticket sales and distribution, maintenance schedules, inventories, as well as financial accounts and personnel records, will all benefit from computerization. This is but one example of the need for staff development which will continue to increase in our rapidly changing society. Employees in management positions may be encouraged or required to take courses in time management, communication skills, risk assessment or whatever new techniques may be beneficial to sports organizations in the future.

§ 1-9. Performance Appraisals.

Performance appraisals are the essence of personnel management. They are the means for evaluating employee effectiveness and a basis for producing change in the work behavior of each employee. The task of assessing performance is a difficult and extremely complex undertaking when all of the organizational and interpersonal ramifications are considered. For these reasons, significant planning and managerial attention should be devoted to the appraisal process.

Performance appraisals are a systematic means for making decisions concerning salary levels, promotions, raises and training needs as well as evaluating ongoing effectiveness of employees. Some organizations require performance appraisals at regular intervals while others allow managers to utilize them at the administrator's discretion. Most often, organizational policies will require a formal performance appraisal prior to any promotion, awarding of merit raises or dismissal of an employee. In every case, they provide the opportunity for employee and supervisor to discuss the employee's job performance and to identify any desired redirection of efforts.

Typically, performance ratings have been developed based on personality traits and work habits, job behaviors or job results. Regardless of the essential focus, current law requires that performance appraisals be based on job-relevant criteria, and not on unrelated personal characteristics or vague items not related to job performance. For example, if appearance and dress are to be used as a rating item, the organization should be able to defend the reason for this in relation to the job. This might be easily done for a secretary or receptionist, but would be more difficult in the case of a grounds-worker or equipment manager.

§ 1-10. Performance Traits.

Often rating systems have used a generalized trait approach. Typically, traits such as: initiative, dependability, leadership, creativity, judgment and cooperation are rated on some scale using either verbal descriptions (excellent, good, average, poor) or a numerical scale (1-high, 3-moderate, 5-low). This trait format has the advantage of being almost universally useful within a large group of employees performing diverse functions. The results of these appraisals provide some general and often useful information concerning employee performance but, in many cases, the information is a vague generalization, subjectively determined by the supervisor. A rating of average on initiative or low on cooperation may not provide the employee with much useful information to improve his performance.

The trait format does offer a reference point to begin a discussion with an employee in which more specific strengths and weaknesses are specified under each general category. The benefit of this form of appraisal is its universal applicability to all employees and its ease of design and administration. Large organizations such as state universities and those utilizing union workers often use this format for all hourly employees. They are often required in the process for retention, promotions, raises and dismissals.

§ 1-11. Management by Objectives.

One currently popular technique devised to assess the accomplishments of employees in a variety of business and educational settings is termed management by objectives. This system incorporates the setting of specific goals or objectives to be accomplished, specifies an appropriate time frame and evaluates staff effectiveness based on the degree of goal attainment. The management-by-objectives format serves to focus the employee's efforts on what management considers to be the most important functions (objectives) and emphasizes measurable results as the basis for success. (Example is located in Appendix 2 at the end of this chapter.) This focus on objectives is a valuable planning tool and serves to control extraneous efforts in which employees might otherwise engage. It allows for the supervisor and employee to jointly agree on the desired accomplishments. Management by objectives does not deal directly with the employee's specific behaviors or the means that may be used to accomplish the objectives. Rather, desirable goals are identified and the employee is allowed the freedom of various means of achieving these goals. Often an employee, such as an assistant coach or fund-raiser, may appear busy all the time with piles of work, but in reality, little is actually accomplished. Management by objectives forces the employee to focus on the end results, the accomplishments.

Management by objectives entails three essential steps:

1. *Setting of objectives:* A meeting of the employee and the manager is conducted to discuss specific objectives to be accomplished. The employee is an important part of the planning process and should be actively involved in setting reasonable objectives. The end result of the meeting is specification of a number of objectives to be accomplished and a rank or priority for each. In addition, a specific time frame is identified for accomplishment and measurable indicators of success are specified.

2. *Provision of time and resources:* A reasonable period of time is allowed with the freedom to pursue the goals as the employee deems most suitable. This has the advantage of often producing substantial creativity and commitment from many workers. Reasonable resources are made available to enable accomplishment of the objectives.

3. *Performance review:* Quantitative and qualitative accomplishment of the objectives are reviewed at specified intervals. Areas of success and failure are noted and new objectives are developed or redefined to provide continued progress toward the larger goal.

Management by objectives may be most applicable to professional-level employees where greater freedom exists in time schedules and resources and where employees have the freedom to initiate new techniques and approaches. This technique provides a clear agreement between the employee and the manager as to the relative importance of the various job tasks and how success in each will be measured.

By focusing exclusively on outcomes, the management-by-objectives approach provides little guidance as to how to accomplish the desired outcomes. New employees may lack sufficient knowledge of how these might be accomplished, what resources are available and what behaviors are ethically or legally acceptable in the organization. Workers may adopt a "results at any cost" approach, where significant damage is done in the process of accomplishing the goal. In most sport organizations, the way the organization treats the public is often at least as important as an ultimate goal of winning or increasing profits. In these situations where alumni or fan identification with the team is of great importance, care must be exercised not to produce some short-term gain at the expense of a long-term loss in support. One method to reduce this undesirable consequence is to review the planned techniques for goal attainment with the supervisor. The employee still has the freedom and exercises the creativity of suggesting means for goal attainment, but approval for using these means must be obtained from supervisors.

§ 1-12. Behaviorally Anchored Rating Systems.

Another technique used to appraise employee performance which focuses on the actual job behaviors has been termed "behaviorally anchored rating systems." This system assesses the employee's performance as a series of on-the-job behaviors. This is in contrast to the management-by-objectives approach of looking at outcomes of job behavior. In the behaviorally anchored system, a set of specific statements describing desirable job behaviors is prepared. These statements describe different levels of job performance in rather specific terms which identify indicators of outstanding performance, good performance, average performance, below average performance and very poor performance. (Example is located in Appendix 3 at the end of this chapter.)

Qualitative statements describing differing levels of job performance are created for each major function or dimension of the employee's assigned tasks. An employee having seven major job functions would have a set of descriptive statements ranging from outstanding through very poor for each of these functions. These sets of behavioral indicators must be developed for each different job classification since obviously, a secretary is not expected to exhibit the same job behaviors that are appropriate to a concessions manager.

This approach to appraising job performance is similar to the current United States Tennis Association (USTA) method of ranking tennis-playing ability. For each of the USTA ranks from 1.0 through 7.0, a set of descriptive statements detailing the player's ability to consistently make various strokes and implement specific strategies is provided. Any player, coach or professional can then attempt to match these statements with the observed level of play to determine which rank best describes the current level of the player.

Similarly, supervisors using a behaviorally anchored rating system observe their employees and determine which set of descriptive statements best depicts each employee's typical performance. This rating is conducted for each of the major dimensions of the employee's job. Thus, a ticket office employee might receive a high rating on personal contact with customers, a low rating on financial record keeping and an average rating for speed of customer service. Each of these dimensions would have a set of statements describing what behaviors are typical of high, average and low performance.

The construction of behaviorally anchored rating systems can be quite time-consuming depending upon the degree of detail desired and the number of different job categories existing within the organization. They do provide an excellent means of feedback to the employee on areas of job performance needing attention and provide descriptive examples of what constitutes the desired behaviors.

Each of the previously described performance appraisal techniques offers specific advantages and entails limitations. The performance-traits approach identifies broad categories of desired traits of all workers and is useful as a general evaluation technique. The management-by-objectives approach focuses on identifying goals and directly assessing progress toward those goals. The clearly described, desirable behavior of workers is the essence of the behaviorally anchored rating system. Competent managers should be familiar with each of these personnel-appraisal techniques and should select appropriate methods which will best serve their specific employees and organization.

All formal performance appraisals should become a part of the personnel file of each employee. This record documents progress or lack of progress and should be reviewed prior to each new appraisal.

The concluding portion of each performance appraisal should include a conference during which the employee and supervisor discuss the contents of the ratings assigned and either reaffirm or redirect specific employee behavior. In some organizations the employee must sign indicating his/her knowledge of the contents of the appraisal. This process offers protection for both the employee and employer should questions of retention, salary adjustment, and other factors be raised at a later date.

The conference should be viewed as a means for staff development. It is essential in providing directions for improved employee performance. Without this feedback the employees may remain essentially unaware of weaknesses in their job performance. The conclusion of the appraisal conference should always communicate confidence in the employee's ability and a helpful attitude on the part of the supervisor.

§ 1-13. Motivating Employees.

Position descriptions and performance appraisals detail the essence of each employee's expected behavior and position in the hierarchy of the organization. Fulfillment of these expectations requires employees to be motivated toward their successful accomplishment. Thus, understanding factors which affect employee motivation is essential in personnel management.

Managers often adopt one of two opposing views of the basic nature of employees. The first holds that employees are: interested in their work, take pride in accomplishments, expend a high degree of effort, are committed to the organization, are ready to accept responsibility and generally exercise good self-control and self-direction. The opposing position describes employees as: basically lazy, lacking in self-direction, working only for money, resistant to change, self-centered and uncooperative.

Obviously, neither depicts an accurate picture of all employees. However, there is some validity in each set of descriptions. There are employees who are quite positive in their approach to their assigned duties and others who are far more negative. Managers would obviously like to have an entire staff consisting of employees possessing the positive qualities. This possibility is enhanced by managers who adopt a positive expectation of each employee. These managers communicate in all their actions that they believe in and expect competent and reliable job performance. Employees sense this positive expectation and, in most cases, aspire to fulfill this role.

Positive managers also understand that an organization works most effectively when employees can satisfy their individual needs while at the same time fulfilling the organizational goals. People work to satisfy a variety of personal needs. Paramount among these are the existence needs: those related to sufficient salary to provide for housing, clothing, food and other essential materials. Once these needs are satisfied on at least an acceptable level, needs for social affiliation and personal accomplishment become of primary concern. Opportunities to fulfill these needs are the motivating factors which are available in the work environment.

Motivating factors can be classified into organizational factors and individual factors. Organizational factors are those which are provided through affiliation with the larger work unit. The most obvious of these are salary and fringe benefits. Additional organizational factors affecting motivation include the desirability of the work environment, the amount of job security, affiliation with the organization and acceptance by co-workers. Individual factors motivating job performance include the opportunity to achieve, to receive recognition, to feel pride, to work autonomously, to obtain intrinsic pleasure from the job and to provide a challenge. In situations where the work is redundant and offers little challenge and few opportunities for self-expression, the major motivation must come from organizational motivational factors. Attractive salary and benefit packages, pleasant office furnishings, up-to-date equipment, positive social climate and reasonable job security make these jobs more desirable and thus motivate employees to attempt to hold their jobs. The individual motivating factors, all related to self-esteem and accomplishment, however, are the more powerful factors for affecting most employee performance. Many employees actively seek new opportunities which provide challenges and the means to achieve promotions, status, acclaim and power, even if these are not directly associated with salary increases.

The individual nature of human behavior necessitates that supervisors understand that each employee is a unique person motivated by a different array of organizational and individual factors. The more familiar managers are with their employees, the better able they are to provide the incentives which will be important to that employee.

Employee motivation is directly influenced by the respect they hold for their supervisors. An ineffectual, unrespected manager produces a work climate fostering uninspired employees. Several suggestions for positive supervision leading to motivated employees include:

1. *Accept the responsibility of the administrator.* Make the decisions which are necessary and take the credit and blame for those decisions. Employees are frustrated when decisions which directly affect them are avoided or unnecessarily delayed. Never allow an employee to shoulder the blame for a decision which was made by the administrator.

2. *Delegate both responsibility and the authority to accomplish assigned tasks.* Allow employees some freedom and creativity in their means of accomplishing their duties.

3. *Give credit for staff accomplishments.* Never allow the misconception to remain that an employee's achievements or ideas were those of the administrator.

4. *Be an understanding supervisor.* Attempt to see situations from the employee's perspective. Be sensitive to what is happening in his total job and life at that moment in time.

All managers must remember that they are responsible for a job far too big for them to accomplish alone. They can only achieve success through effectively motivating others to perform the necessary job tasks.

Occasionally it is necessary to reprimand an employee. This can be thought of as negative motivation. Typically threats, corrections, and expressions of displeasure are necessary either to ensure acceptable employee behavior or to communicate expressions of inadequate performance.

Reprimands should be factually based and directed at the act or behavior, not at the individual's personality. Statements such as "you are a poor worker," "you have no commitment to the organization," "you just don't measure up" or "you are a poor reflection of our team" attack the person rather than the undesirable behavior. Attempts to describe the specific behavior as undesirable usually prove more productive. Some examples might be: "we expect all our staff to be at their work site by 8:00 a.m."; "office staff shall refer all questions from the media to the sport information office; never comment on player-coach conflicts." These statements focus the criticism on the behavior rather than the personality of the employee. The tone and emotionality of the reprimand should be sincere, controlled and factual. Often reference to policy, procedures or job specifications is all that is necessary to remind employees of their expected performance. It is unnecessary and often unproductive to "blow-up" or show excessive emotionality.

Reprimands should generally be given in private. They should be rather short in duration but should allow the employees an opportunity to express their side of the issue. Often it is a desirable practice to begin by asking the employee to explain the situation from his viewpoint. Once the reprimand has been given, the supervisor should not hold the incident against the employee on future occasions unless the same mistake is repeated. The manager might wish to monitor the recently reprimanded behavior with the goal of reinforcing the new, desired behavior, when it is exhibited. This will help solidify this behavior and provide the employee with the feeling that the supervisor does notice when the job is done correctly.

§ 1-14. Personnel Records.

A personnel file should be established as a depository for all pertinent information concerning the employment status and productivity of each employee. These files serve the purpose of recording all aspects of employment status including: position title, contract provisions, an accounting of benefits, accumulated sick leave and vacation time. The files often also include sufficient personal information to enable the organization to contact the employee at home, to notify his physician, spouse or next of kin in an emergency and to complete required social security, income tax and other salary-oriented financial matters.

The personnel file may also serve as a record of the employee's significant accomplishments, and as a documentation of any disciplinary actions which may have been taken. This latter use is especially important when justification may be required in a case of dismissal. Normally all official performance appraisals should become a part of the employee's personnel file.